Refinish Old Furniture

T N van der Walt

Copyright © 2012 T N van der Walt

All rights reserved.

ISBN:1533573603
ISBN-13:978153373605

LEGAL NOTICE

While the author has attempted to be as accurate and complete as possible, he assumes no responsibility for errors, omissions or contrary interpretation of the subject matter.

This book is not intended for use as a source of legal, business or financial advice.

Any earnings or income statements are only estimates of what the author thinks you can earn. There is no assurance that you will achieve this income. The financial figures in this book are illustrative only and do not necessarily reflect the real prices and value of products.

You are NOT licensed to resell, loan, give away or auction this book without the specific written consent of the author.

All rights reserved.

CONTENTS

	Legal notice	i
1	Refinishing furniture as a business	5
2	Tool and equipment required	7
3	Stripping old finish	17
4	Repairs	23
5	How to apply paint and other finishes	25
6	Paint techniques	45
7	How to grow your business	59
8	Resources	74
	Conclusion	77

CHAPTER 1 - REFINISHING FURNITURE AS A BUSINESS

1.1 Profitable home business

There will always be a good market for quality refinished furniture. This is an ideal home business and can be started with minimum capital outlay. The skills needed to re-finish furniture can also be easily acquired and with some practice, a professional finish can be achieved. There are some basic requirements that have to be met if you want to succeed in this home business. The first is that you should have a reasonable size space available to do the stripping and painting. A double garage is ideal to start off with. The painting area and the stripping and prepping area should be kept separate as far as possible. Secondly, some basic tools and equipment will be necessary but these can be bought at reasonable prices at any good hardware shop. Thirdly, a market must be developed and this will take some time. However, you can start small and gradually grow your business because you will have virtually no overheads and all the input costs can be derived from your client at the start of a project.

Maybe it sounds over simplified, but I have gone through the process and my experience was that the business just had a steady growth right from the start. The most important aspect is to provide a trustworthy and quality service. Remember, anyone can make a mistake but the crucial point is that mistakes must be rectified quickly and without any arguments. The old cliché of the client that is always right is a golden rule that will serve you well. There are no short cuts in the refinishing business. The processes that I will describe later on, have all been tried and tested by many people in this business, and must be applied without any attempts to bypass or manipulate. This will enable you to be successful in this business.

Refinishing implies that you take an old piece of furniture and strip the old finishing (varnish, paint etc.) and refinish it by re-varnishing or painting the piece. However, before you can do that you may first have to remove hardware such as handles and there may also be a need to do minor repairs. When mayor repairs are needed, it is best to get it done by an expert. Remember, you are not in the business of furniture making or restoration.

Refinishing as a home business requires that you not only have the skill to refinish, but also to operate as a business. This means that you must be able to make a profit and to do this you must know how to determine the price that you will charge for your work. This is an important aspect and I have developed a system that will assist you and in chapter 7 you will find more information.

1.2 Skills and training required

Refinishing does not require special skills and if you have a general knowledge of wood work and painting you will pick up the rest as you go along. The most difficult part is to master the technique of spray painting but also in this case, it can be acquired easily with a bit of practice. In chapter 5 you will get more on the technique of spray painting. It will obviously be of great benefit to have training as a carpenter and or a spray painter but I have neither and have quickly mastered the techniques.

CHAPTER 2 - TOOLS AND EQUIPMENT REQUIRED

If you want to develop a successful home business, you should aim to be as professional as possible. For this reason I recommend that you spray paint where possible to get a professional finish. For this you will require the following equipment:

Spray gun

Air compressor

Mixing tools such as measuring cups and mixing paddle

Safety equipment such as a good respirator and safety glasses

Other tools and equipment include:

Sanding equipment such as a hand orbital sander and belt sander

Paint brushes, rollers and paint scrapers

Hand tools such as screw driver, hammer, pliers etc

Power tools such as drill, planer, power saw etc.

2.1 Spray guns

A spray gun is the only tool that will give you a professional finish. It will give a really smooth finish whereas brushes and rollers always leave marks. There are two common types of spray guns used in finishing:

• Conventional (low volume/high pressure) spray guns work with compressed air and blast the finish onto the wood at 3 – 5.0 bar. The gun's air consumption is 4 – 7 cubic feet per minute (cfm). A high pressure gun will generally give a smoother finish than a HVLP gun.

- HVLP (high volume/low pressure) spray guns work with either compressed air or turbine air and lay the finish onto the wood softly at 2.5 – 3.5 bars. Air consumption is rated at 4 – 6 CFM. These guns create much less overspray.

Conventional Spray Guns (LVHP)

Conventional spray guns have been used for a long time. They provide excellent control of the liquid material that reaches the surface. But they have one serious drawback - they are only about 20 to 30 percent efficient. This means that well over half of the material you're spraying is wasted - it goes into the air.

High Volume Low Pressure Spray Guns (HVLP)

HVLP spray guns were developed more than 30 years ago but are only recently becoming popular. HVLP guns can work with either compressed air or continuous air supplied by a turbine. Either way, the result is a low pressure spray that creates very little overspray. HVLP guns are 65 to 90 percent efficient, which means that most of the material you're spraying ends up on the wood. There are two advantages to using a turbine over a compressor with an HVLP spray gun:

- A turbine passes a high volume of air directly to the gun at about 4 psi. A compressor generates much higher pressure at lower volume. In order to raise the volume enough to operate the HVLP gun, the high-pressure air must be sent through a regulator. This transforms the high pressure to high volume and low pressure. It takes a large, expensive 3- to 5-horsepower compressor to adequately supply an HVLP gun, compared to a small, inexpensive turbine.

- Turbines warm and dry the air, which speeds curing and helps reduce blushing (a moisture-related, off-white color that appears as some finishes cure).

To get started a HVLP gun with a 1.8 or 2.0 mm nozzle is ideal. To do touch up work a smaller gun with a 1.0 mm nozzle will also be needed.

2.2 Compressors

To start off with I would suggest that a smaller compressor be acquired. A minimum tank capacity of 50 L is required and should preferably be belt driven. It should be driven by a motor of at least 2 hp or 1.5 kW. An air delivery rate of minimum 6 cfm (cubic feet per minute) and maximum pressure of 8 bars or 116 psi (pounds per square inch) is needed. This size compressor will easily handle most HVLP guns.

Should the volume of work increase, a bigger more expensive compressor can be bought and the smaller compressor can be used as stand-by or used for on-site jobs.

There are also two advantages to using a compressor over a turbine:

• A compressor that is large enough (2-5 horsepower or larger) can generate more pressure at the gun than do commonly available turbines-up to 10 psi. This results into more finish material being deposited onto the wood surface at a faster rate. The increase allows you to coat an object in less time. Turbine supplied HVLP spray guns don't put out as much material as compressor-supplied HVLP guns or, for that matter, compressor supplied conventional guns.

• A compressor can be used for other shop tasks, such as powering compressed-air woodworking tools and blowing dust off your work. Turbines are ineffective at these tasks

2.3 Mixing and tools and equipment

Spray painting requires that the paint be accurately mixed so that you get the correct consistency – not too thick and not too thin. Most paint manufacturers give an indication of the ratio of solvent to the paint volume required. As a rule of thumb, 10% solvent is usually sufficient. However, some water based paints are non-drip and comes as a thick liquid that will require a bigger ratio – up to 15%.

Mixing cups are available in the paint trade. These are ideal for accurately measuring the paint mix. Different sizes are available but the 1 liter cups are the most practical. A spray painter's ruler is also a handy measurement and mixing tool.

Most paints used for spray painting must be filtered to get rid of small particles. Paint strainers of various grid sizes are available but the medium mesh size is preferable. Clean paint prevents clogging of nozzles and air holes on the paint gun. Paper strainers can be cleaned and used two or three times before discarding. Reusable paint strainers are also available.

Clean rag cloths is another essential in the paint shop.

2.4 Safety equipment

Spray painting can be hazardous to your health and it is important that you take steps to avoid unnecessary exposure to fumes, overspray, chemicals and dust. Apart from making sure that the spray area is properly ventilated, the following equipment is required:

2.4.1 Respirator

Respirators come in a wide range of types and sizes.

They range from cheaper disposable types to reusable types that make use of replaceable filtering cartridges.

The two main categories are:

Air purifying respirator (APR)

Air supplied respirator (SAR)

APR's forces contaminated air through a cartridge filter that contains an absorbing material such as carbon and the gases and fumes are absorbed. They are tight fitting and are available in different forms:

Quarter mask – covers nose and mouth

Half – face mask – covers face from the nose to below the chin

Full face mask – covers face from the eyes to below the chin. It protects the eyes from dust and fumes

SAR's supply clean air from a compressed air tank. The air from a tank must comply with standards for purity and moisture. These systems are mostly used in industrial applications and are expensive. For a home business the half- or full-face masks are more than adequate.

The best filter to use is the chemical cartridge respirators that have a combination of chemicals and a dust filter.

Filters must be checked regularly to make sure it does not become clogged. Cartridges have a limited life span and must be replaced when they become saturated. It will stop working and the vapors will pass through the filter and can be smelled or tasted. The best is to follow the manufacturer's recommendations. The 3M respirators are expensive but to my mind the best that you can get. The filter is made up of carbon particles that absorb different types of vapors and gasses. These particles will become "saturated" after a while and cartridges must be replaced:

When the paint can be smelled or tasted

When used on a regular basis, they must be replaced after 40 hours use

When opened (even if not used) they must be replaced after 6 months

When the expiry date on the cartridge is reached.

There are different types of filters or cartridges and the main ones are:

N series – non-resistant to oil

R series – resistant to oil

P series – oil-proof

Cartridges can be identified by the color of the container.

Table 1 – Types of cartridge

Filter type	Color code	Description
A	Orange	Organic vapors and gasses
B	Grey	Inorganic vapors and gasses
E	Yellow	Acid vapors and gasses

K	Green	Ammonia vapors and gasses
ABEK	Combination of above	Combination filter for all above
P	White	Dust/Particle removal

Recommendation:

I suggest that you use the 3 M half mask respirator with the orange/brown organic gas and vapor cartridge (A type). Replace the dust filters regularly and depending on the frequency of use of the mask, or when the filter becomes soiled.

With a half mask you should also wear safety glasses. Special glasses that fit over the mask are available in the trade.

2.5 Brushes and Rollers

2.5.1 Brushes

Good quality paint brushes of different sizes will be needed for touch up work, cleaning of dust from the wood etc.

There are basically three types of brushes. Natural hair brushes, synthetic brushes and sponge brushes. Pad applicators can also be regarded as brushes.

The difference between natural and synthetic brushes is like the difference between hair and plastic. Hair becomes uncontrollable when it gets wet but plastic remains workable. It is for this *Natural hair bristle* brushes are preferred for oil based paint and varnishes. *Foam and sponge brushes* are popular because they do not leave brush marks. However, to get a really smooth finish they must be used carefully but with some practice they will give a good result. *Synthetic brushes* are the most versatile of lot and provided that you get a high quality brush, they can be used to get a good finish.

2.5.2 Rollers

Sponge rollers are becoming increasingly popular because they do not leave marks and will give a smooth finish. They are used on flat surfaces but are not effective on round surfaces and edges. To get a smooth finish the roller must be used in one direction only. Do not roll back and forth on the same stroke – rather pick up the roller and start the second stroke from the beginning and roll in one direction.

2.6 Workshop tables

To facilitate with the refinishing process there are some accessories that you can make yourself. The first that you will need are saw horses to place the work piece. It is suggested that you use ordinary builders Pine wood. To produce one saw horse you will need the following:

>Five lengths of 500 mm 110 mm x 38 mm

>Nails 60 mm

>Ordinary pine planks of between 2 and 3 meters, 320 mm x 38 mm (used by builders as scaffold planks) to put on the work horses for a work surface.

To start off with it is suggested that you should have at least 4 saw horses and 4 planks. A proper work bench is also required. This is needed as a work surface to mix paint, clean equipment etc.

2.7 Stripping tools and equipment

Stripping tools are essential for the preparation of the wood surface. It is rare not to strip or sand the old finish before painting. The following are the most important tools:

2.7.1 Sanders

The following types of sanders are available:

Belt sanders remove a lot of material and must be used with caution. It will leave heavy sanding marks and will need further sanding with an orbital sander and finer sand paper.

Orbital sanders are not as aggressive but also do not remove a lot of material. It still leaves orbital scratches and must be smoothed down with finer grit sand paper. It is only effective when the old finish has started flaking and has dried out completely.

Random orbital sanders have a revolving as well as an orbital movement. They are more effective than orbital sanders and much more effective in removing old finish. This is the best option for most sanding operations.

2.7.2 Heat gun

Two types are available - flame and heat blower. Care must be taken when using a heat gun because it can easily burn the wood and leave burn marks. It is also a messy process and will not entirely remove old finish.

2.7.3 Sand paper

Sandpaper comes in different grades. The grade is based on the number of abrasive particles per square inch that make up the sandpaper. The lower the number, the coarser the grit.

Coarse – 40 to 60 grit   Medium – 80 to 120 grit

Fine – 150 to 180 grit   Very fine – 220 to 240 grit

Extra fine – 280 to 320 grit Super fine – 360 and above

Garnet paper is usually a brownish-red or yellow color, which is commonly used in woodworking. It will not sand wood as quickly as other sandpapers, but leaves a better finish. Garnet is an excellent choice for finish sanding.

Aluminum Oxide is another common type of sandpaper for woodworking projects. It is the type of paper most often used in power sanders. Aluminum Oxide is more durable than Garnet paper, but doesn't leave as nice of a finish.

Silicon Carbide paper is typically a dark gray or even black. This type of paper is used primarily for finishing metals or for "wet-sanding", using water as a lubricant. While some advanced finishes use Silicon Carbide paper, it is not typically used in woodworking.

When sanding flat surfaces it is much easier to use a sanding block to get an even finish.

CHAPTER 3 - STRIPPING OLD FINISH

There are a number of ways to strip the old paint or varnish finish from wood.

Strip by sanding by hand or a sander

Strip with chemical stripper

Strip with heat.

3.1 Sanding

Sanding to remove old finish or to prepare the wood for painting is an important step in the refinishing process. It is important to use the correct sand paper. A wrong choice can damage the wood surface and make it difficult to repair.

The general approach to sanding is to start with a coarser grit and then move to a finer grit to remove grit marks left by the coarser sandpaper.

Sanding can be done mechanically or by hand. Mechanical sanding is sometimes unavoidable. Small area such as arm rests, table legs and edges must be sanded by hand.

When sanding flat areas by hand it is always better to use a sanding block - always sand in the direction of the wood grain. Once the old finish has been removed, the wood must be smoothed with finer sand paper. I like to start sanding with a 150 grit, then move to 220 grit to smooth the wood grain.

When buying sand paper, be aware that you can get dry and wet paper. For paint removal the dry paper seems to be more effective. The cabinet paper in orange is mostly used on wood.

3.2 Chemical stripper

This is the most efficient way of stripping old paint or varnishes. There are two types available – solvent based and water based. The water based stripper has many advantages over the oil based strippers. Some of these are:

Does not severely irritate the skin or eyes

Equipment can be cleaned with water

I prefer to use Plascon's *Remove All* stripper. It is effective and has virtually no odor. It can easily be washed off with water. It has the following features:

A thick gel formulation that clings to vertical surfaces.

Bio degradable.

Water based.

Non flammable.

Contains no ethylene chloride.

Safe, effective, and easy to use.

It is a South African product and obtainable at Plascon paint dealers. Just follow the instructions on the container and you can't go wrong. You might have to repeat the process a few times by brushing the liquid on and after 10 – 20 minutes scraping it off. When the process is finished, the stripper must be neutralized by rinsing it down with sugar soap and water. I use a pot scraper to wash down and remove the remaining patches of paint. When the wood is completely dry you can start with the sanding process. You might find that the wood grain has been raised and to rectify this, the wood must first be treated with a sanding sealer and then sanded down to a smooth finish.

Remember that all chemical strippers can be harmful to your

health. So it's best to use gloves, eye protection and a suitable mask.

Stripping of old finish is a most important step in the process of refinishing. If you do not do this properly, the end result will be bad and in most cases this means that you have to start the process all over again. Once the old paint or varnish is removed the next step is to sands it to a smooth finish – as smooth as possible. Therefore, start with 220 grit sanding paper and finish off with 880 or even 1000 grit. Wipe dust completely and inspect for sanding marks or other blemishes that may remain.

There is another option which does not involve stripping the old finish before you start painting. Provided that the existing finish is still in good shape and does not crack, peel or make bubbles, take the following steps:

Clean the wood by washing with sugar soap to remove dirt and grease. Wash down with clean water and let it dry.

Sand lightly with 220 grit sandpaper

Seal the wood with a clear water based sealer such as Plascon's Glaze Coat

When dry, paint with water based paint.

This process is especially successful where the old finish is oil based paint or any lacquer or varnish finish. When you do not seal it first, the water based paint over the oil based paint will result in yellow stains that may appear. This is due to the oil seeping through and staining the paint. To resolve this problem, you can seal the paint and then repaint in the surface again. This should remove the stains.

3.3 Using Heat Guns

Basically there are two tools available for stripping paint with heat – heat gun and blow torch. The main difference is that the blow torch has an open flame whereas the heat gun heats air that is blown over the wood.

Blow torches are much more aggressive and must be used with care to avoid scourging or burning the wood.

When using either tool ensure that it is held a constant distance from the surface, roughly 6 to 8 inches from the surface. Move the gun backwards and forwards in a sweeping motion. Do not keep the gun stationery on one spot to avoid overheating and scourging the wood. When the paint starts to wrinkle and lift from the surface, it must be removed with a paint scraper. Keep an old container such as an empty tin handy to discard the melted paint.

Repeat the process until all the paint is removed. Use a 220 grit sand paper to remove remaining paint residue and make sure that the surface is clean and smooth before painting.

Remember that the heat can be dangerous when it comes in contact with flammable substances such as thinners. Oil based paints may also give off harmful gases and it is preferable to use a mask, gloves and eye protection.

Advantages:

Can remove paint very quickly

Works on multiple layers

Relatively cheap to purchase

Disadvantages:

Can be very dangerous

Can damage the surface or item you are trying to strip especially wood surfaces

May need several different tools to complete the job.

Use heat stripping with care and unless manual sanding or electric sanders are unsuccessful, try and avoid heat gins.

CHAPTER 4 - REPAIRS

More often than not, old pieces of furniture need at least minor repairs. In some cases parts are broken so badly that it must be replaced. Making new parts cannot be considered part of the refinishing process. This should be left to furniture makers.

Before any repairs can be done all hardware should be removed – locks, handles hinges and metal beadings. Next the item should be properly cleaned. If necessary, a solution of warm water and sugar soap should be used the wash down the wood. Use a firm brush to remove grease and dirt. Rinse with clean water and let the wood dry out completely before working on it. Next repairs can be done.

4.1 Fixing cracks and holes

Sometimes cracks may occur and depending on the extent it affects the construction of the piece, can be prepared with wood glue and clamping it for a few hours. If the crack is small, it can be fixed with wood filler. Fill up higher than the surrounding surface and sand down when dry. When the item must be varnished rather than painted, wood filler can be problematic because the color seldom matches the original finish. Try to get some wood shavings that match the original finish and mix with wood glue. Insert it into the crack and when it is dry, sand to a smooth finish.

Where bigger crack or chips in the wood must be filled, it is best to use a wood epoxy such as Quick Wood. It can also be sanded to a fine finish and will not chip or wear off.

4.2 Repairing drawers

In many old cabinets the drawers do not work properly and this can in most cases fixed without major effort. The mechanism for opening a drawer can include rollers (mostly in kitchen cabinets), runners at the bottom of the drawer and a groove on the sides of the drawer that accommodates a wooden guide that runs in the opening.

Most common problems found in drawers are the following:

Drawer keeps sliding out

Won't close properly

Drawer bottom is sagging or broken

Drawer frame joints loose

Drawer won't slide

When a drawer keeps falling out it usually do not have a stop at the back of the drawer. To fix the problem, cut a piece of hardwood and fasten it to the back of the drawer. Swing it away to insert the drawer and then fix the stop block with a second nail or screw.

Drawers that do not want to close or get stuck can have several problems such as:

Loose joints

Drawers are put together by using dovetail joints or butt joints. Dovetail joints seldom separate. If they do become loose, force some wood glue into the joint and clamp firmly together. Butt joints usually need more attention. Try and take the joint apart and after cleaning it properly, glue and clamp. If possible you can nail the joint to give extra strength.

Sticky drawers

This can be caused by the runners that may need lubricating with stick lubricant, candle wax or silicone sprays. Do not use ordinary oil since it collects dust and worsens the problem. If lubrication does not help, sand the down the binding points. Seal the raw wood with shellac to prevent future swelling.

Worn guides and runners

Wood or metal runners are used to guide drawers to move in and out. When they are worn or splintering they must be smoothed out with sandpaper or they must be replaced. Metal guides that can be bought at any hardware store can be installed. You could also replace the runners with new wooden runners. Use hardwood to make the runner. Secure it with glue and nails. Countersink the nails to so they won't interfere with the drawer's movement.

Worn drawer bottoms

Drawer bottoms are fixed to the frame by slots in the sides of the drawer into which the bottom slides in loosely. To replace a drawer bottom, remove one end of the drawer and slide out the bottom panel. Replace it with new hardboard or hardwood panel cut to size.

Some drawer bottoms are secured with moldings or corner blocks at the inside edges of the sides and back of the drawer. Remove these before taking out the bottom.

Fixing legs on chairs and tables

When a leg is broken, it is difficult to repair and most of the time should be replaced with a new leg. However, when the leg joint is loose, it can be repaired by taking the joints apart and then re-gluing the joints. Alternatively, a dowel can be inserted to connect the leg with the adjoining part of the table. Corner blocks can also be fastened in the corners under the table top to strengthen the joint of the leg to the table frame.

CHAPTER 5 - HOW TO APPLY PAINT AND OTHER FINISHES

Applying the paint or other finish such as varnish, takes some practice to achieve a professional result. The best method of applying paint is the use of a spray gun. The spray technique can easily be mastered, provided that the right procedures are followed.

5.1 How to spray paint.

Proper spraying techniques are very logical. Some of the basic principles for quality spraying are the following:

Plan a systematic spraying routine that will reduce waste and overspray. I start on the underside of a piece of furniture. On a chair for instance, tip it over and start with the legs and the bottom. Then turn it over and start from the top by spraying the back, armrests etc. Lastly spray the seat. Always work from top to bottom and the inside to the outside. Work from the less visible to the more visible areas.

Make sure that you have adequate light. After spraying, look against the light to see areas that do not have enough paint. The surface must be shiny after spraying.

Keep the spray gun pointed perpendicular to the surface of the wood. Avoid movements of the wrist. Move the whole arm from left to right.

Set your gun to a fan pattern that covers the surface with the fewest passes and the least overspray. Use a small fan pattern on edges, rails, turnings, and other narrow surfaces. Use a wide fan pattern on large, wide surfaces.

Start spraying about 4 -6 inches from to the side of the wood, and move the spray onto the wood. Keep moving at a uniform speed.

Keep the gun a uniform distance from the surface of the wood between 6 and 10 inches. If you move it too close, you will make runs; move it too far away, and you will have dry spray. You usually have to hold an HVLP gun several inches closer to the wood than you do a conventional gun.

Finish your stroke several inches past the edge of the wood. Make it a habit to release the trigger of the gun at the end of each stroke.

Make sure that the strokes overlap to ensure even thickness. Also spray each stroke at least two times - one stroke to the edge and back on the same stroke. Overlap each previous stroke by half. This will give an even thickness overall.

Avoid spraying to much the first time around. Running of the paint may occur and then you will have to redo the whole process. Rather spray several coats to make sure you have adequate coverage.

Remember, practice makes perfect. Don't expect to be an expert spray painter after the first couple of efforts.

First spray a test stroke on a piece of scrap to make sure the spray pattern is correct and the volume of air and material is adequate. After spraying a few strokes, stop spraying and stand away and have a look against the light to see if the painted surface is shiny and that it does not appear like a matt finish. If the latter is the case, not enough paint is deposited and it must be corrected by doing one of the following:

Make sure the paint is not too thick and the volume of air and paint release is sufficient.

Make sure the paint nozzle on the gun is open and not blocked by impurities.

Close the paint volume knob and spray to remove impurities. If this does not help, the cup must be emptied and the gun taken apart and cleaned.

5.1.2 Mixing the paint

Another important skill that is required for proper spraying is the ability to properly mix the paint. In most cases the commercial paints are thick (especially water based paint) and need to be thinned to achieve a good flow of paint through the gun. Mixing takes a bit of practice. Water based paint can be thinned up to 10% or even more. A paint measuring cup clearly indicates the 10% scale and should preferably be used. A spray painter's ruler can also be used. Always spray a test stroke to make sure that the right amount of paint is deposited.

Most Acrylic paints must be thinned down to get the right consistency (thickness). In most cases adding 10% of the solvent (water, mineral turpentine or thinners) will be adequate. However, depending on the brand of paint you might have to do some experimenting to achieve the right consistency.

After thinning, the paint must be filtered through a paint strainer to remove impurities. There are different types of strainers but the most popular are nylon mesh or paper funnel strainers.

Tip: *You can make your own reusable paint strainer from the same strainer material that can be bought from a paint dealer. The 20 liter strainer can be cut up into smaller pieces to fit around the mixing cup. Use a piece of elastic to secure the mesh over the cup. Pour the paint and then detach and wash the mesh for future use.*

5.1.3 Set the spray gun to the correct setting

Always make sure that you have the correct setting on your gun for the amount of air that goes through the nozzle. The combination of air and paint is called atomization. The gun shoots a stream of paint that is broken up in a mist of tiny droplets that is deposited on the wood. If you have too little air, the atomization won't be great enough, and the finish won't flow together. It will cure looking like the surface of an orange; the effect is called orange peel. If you have too much air, the finish will dry before it hits the wood, producing a dusty look. This is called dry spray.

The two air jets that direct the atomizing air have an additional function. They determine the width of the paint fan by forcing the air on the stream of paint. By increasing the air flow through these jets, you widen the fan, so you can coat a wider area with each pass. By decreasing the airflow, you shrink the fan to a very small circular pattern, which you can use to fill in small defects. By rotating the air nozzle, you can change the angle of the fan relative to the gun.

5.1.4 Organizing the work

When panting furniture it is always best to start with the least visible areas. When painting a chair for instance, turn the chair upside down and first spray the underside and the legs. Let it dry for a few minutes and the turn it over to do the top. When spraying table tops first spray the edges and work towards the more visible areas. Try and handle the work piece as little as possible. Use a work horse and scaffold planks as a bench to place the chair at a convenient height to reach all the difficult places. Let the work piece become touch-dry before you handle it. It is also important to make sure that no dust or insects come into contact with the work piece before the paint is touch-dry.

5.1.5 Maintenance and cleaning

One of the most important aspects in being a good spray painter is to get in the routine of good housekeeping. Always keep the area free of dust. You could even spray water on the floor surface to settle dust. Make sure that the piece is clean and free from dust particles. Run the palm of your hand over the furniture. You will immediately feel dust and rough patches. Get into the habit of wiping the surface with a clean cloth before spraying or even better, use your compressor to blow away dust.

Cleaning paint equipment such as the spray gun is critically important. After each spray session, disassemble the gun totally and clean out with the substance recommended by the paint manufacturer (water, thinners or mineral turpentine). It is especially important with water based paint. Once this paint is cured water will not clean it and thinners will have to be used. If you have a gravity fed gun make sure that you also clean the breathing hole in the lid of the cup.

The following general maintenance plan (table 2) should be followed:

Table 2 - General Preventative Maintenance Plan – Spray Gun

Procedure	Daily	Weekly
1. Fill cup with solvent (water, turpentine or thinners)	X	
Clean with brush. Spray to clean material passage	X	
2. Remove cup and lid. Wipe clean and open vent hole	X	
3. Remove paint needle and clean	X	
4. Remove nozzle cap and nozzle	X	

5. Clean with solvent and blow dry with compressed air	X	
6. Clean gun body with solvent and blow dry with air	X	
7. Oil needle and needle spring		X
8. Oil air intake needle and spring		X
9. Oil threads and hinges		X

When spraying at intervals longer than 1 hour, steps 1 – 6 must be repeated after each spray.

To properly maintain your compressor, the following general maintenance plan should be followed.

Table 3 – Preventative maintenance – air compressors

General Preventive Maintenance Plan - Compressor

Procedure	Daily	Weekly	Monthly	Annually (200 Hours)
Check Pump Oil Level		X		
Oil Leak Inspection	X			
Drain water in tank		X		

Check for weird noise and vibration	X			
Inspect all air leaks	X			
Inspect belts	X			
Check air filters, clean or replace		X		
Check safety relief valve			X	
Check belts if necessary			X	
Check and tighten all bolts			X	
Check connections for leaks			X	
Service pump or engine				X

5.1.6 Where to Spray

You can spray in a garage with the doors open, or outdoors, preferably in the shade when there's a very slight breeze. Or you can spray indoors with an exhaust system to remove the fumes and overspray. The best setup for indoors is a spray booth, which exhausts the air through a filter that catches all the solid finish particles. Don't use a fan in a window unless it is an explosion-proof fan, which has a shielded motor. Otherwise, sparks from the motor might ignite lacquer and varnish fumes; also, the solid particles from your overspray will build up on the fan's electrical components, increasing the fire hazard.

I started off in my garage and within a year I had to get a bigger work place. I approached a local cabinet maker and suggested that I set up a facility at the back of his shop and that I would do spray painting for him. This was agreed and I then bought a second hand ship container and converted it into a spray booth. Although the space is small, it is sufficient for spraying. Other activities such as sanding and washing are still done in the garage.

5.2 Painting old furniture

When dealing with old furniture, the preparation of the wood is even more important than with new furniture. Old furniture is mostly finished with varnishes, lacquer and shellac. Most of these are oil based and therefore, present a problem when applying water based paint. The first step I take when painting an older piece of furniture is determining what type of paint is already on the piece. Is it oil-based or is it water-based?

Determining if it's a water-based or oil product is important because ...

Oil can be painted over water paint BUT water can't be painted over oil. If you try to apply acrylic paint over oil paint, the paint will not adhere properly and yellow marks may show through on the surface!

Once you have determined the type of paint, it helps you to decide on the proper paint and primer that you will need for the project.

Here's a quick and fast way to find out if your piece of furniture is painted in acrylic or oil. This technique will also work on walls, doors, cabinets, baseboards or any other painted surface!

1. Add some rubbing alcohol to a cotton swab or a clean rag.

2. In a discreet area, wipe the surface back and forth with the rubbing alcohol.

3. If the paint starts to rub off and you see white or faded streaks, you know this has been painted with a water-based product.

4. If no paint comes off, then you know it has been painted with oil based products.

As a general rule the following steps should be followed when painting old furniture:

Step 1 – Clean and sand

Mix sugar soap with warm water and wash down the work piece. When dry start to remove old finish. Test with 150 grit sand paper to see if the finish can be removed easily. If not, you might have to use a chemical paint stripper to do the job. Where the old finish is still in a good condition, it is not necessary to remove all the finish. Just remove the gloss and then use a finer sand paper such as 220 grit to smooth down the surface. Wipe the wood with a damp cloth to remove the dust.

Step 2 – Fill cracks and holes

Use wood filler to fill holes and cracks. Bigger holes could be filled with wood epoxy to provide a stronger patch. Sand it to a smooth finish. This step might be repeated when the under coat is applied because small scratches and dents will then be more visible.

Step 3 – Seal and prime

When painting with water based paint, it is important to first seal the wood to avoid yellow stains seeping through when you apply the paint. Use water based clear sealer. When dry, sand with a 220 grit sand paper and then apply a multi-purpose undercoat. The work piece should now be ready to apply the first top coat. Remember to sand the undercoat with 220 grit sand paper.

Step 5– Apply top coats (at least 2)

Water based enamel paint is ideal to use as a furniture paint. Some brands are thicker and are non-drip. Whatever the case, the paint should be thinned with water (10%) to make it easier to apply. Do not try and cover the wood in one thick coat. Rather put on 2 or 3 thinner coats and you will get a much smoother finish. Also remember to sand with 220 grit sand paper between coats.

5.3 Painting new furniture

New furniture does not need sealing but must be primed before painting. With Pine furniture, the wood knots must first be sealed with a knot sealer. This prevents wood oil seeping through to the paint.

With new furniture the following general steps should be followed:

Step 1 – Sand and seal where necessary

Do not skip the sanding even if the wood surface seems smooth. Use a finer grit to get it as smooth as possible. Seal pine wood with knot seal. Sanding sealer can be used to seal timber grain. It is also good grain filler and can be used as a base coat before applying the top coats.

Step 2 – Apply primer and/or universal under coat

Wood primer penetrates and seals the wood. It provides a strong bond for subsequent coats. The disadvantage is that it is slow drying and takes 16 hours before it can be over coated. It is also toxic and must handle with care. Eye and hand protection is necessary as well as good ventilation. I find that in most cases a good undercoat to be sufficient and use a primer only where the wood is very porous but sanding sealer can also do the job.

Universal undercoat acts as a sandwich coat between the primer and Alkyd top coats. It is used on both new wood and previously painted surfaces.

Multi-surface undercoat is water-based and is ideal when used in conjunction with water-based top coats. It is fast drying and contains no lead or harmful chemicals. It can be over coated with Alkyd, vinyl or water-based paints. It can be used on new and previously painted surfaces. I recommend the use of multi-purpose under coat/primer for furniture and cabinets (including Melamine surfaces).

Step 3 – Apply top coats

This is the same as for previously painted surfaces. Apply at least two coats and use 220 grit sand paper to sand lightly between coats. After the final coat the work piece must not be handled or moved before it is touch-dry. Make sure that dust does not come into contact with the wet surface.

5.4 Painting kitchen cabinets

5.4.1 New wood cabinets

As will be discussed later, kitchen cabinets (both new and used) can provide a significant financial benefit to your business. Cabinet makers are not really in the paint business and this provides a unique business opportunity for furniture spray painters.

New hardwood cabinets are treated in much the same way as any piece of furniture. The same process is followed. The process starts with preparing the wood by smoothing it to a fine finish first. Then a sanding sealer or primer is applied. The next step is a suitable multi-surface undercoat; where after two top coats are applied.

It is important to use the correct type of paint because it requires a hard wearing paint to withstand rough handling as well as moisture, heat and scratches. Some major paint manufacturers have specific brands for kitchens and bathrooms. Water-based enamel paint is recommended for kitchen cabinets. This is a tough enamel paint that contains a polyurethane hybrid that prevents chipping and peeling. It is scratch resistant and completely washable. It is antibacterial and prevents fungus growth.

5.4.2 Previously painted kitchen cabinets

Refinishing old kitchen cabinets can be very rewarding because it is much cheaper than new cabinets and when done properly, looks great.

The process includes the following steps:

Step 1 – Remove doors and shelves and clean

Remember to number the doors before removing them – putting them back will be much easier. Remove handles and hinges and wash them with a mixture of sugar soap and warm water to remove grease and dirt. Rinse with clean water to neutralize the sugar soap.

Step 2 – Sand old finish

Where the old finish is still in a good condition, it is not necessary to remove it all together but it is necessary to sand it down to a smooth finish and to break the shiny gloss to a matt finish. Start by using a 100 grit sand paper and follow it up with a finer 220 grit.

Step 3 – Apply undercoat

Apply a multi-purpose undercoat. Sand down to a fine finish with 220 grit sandpaper.

Step 4 – Apply top coats

Apply two coats of water-based enamel paint.

5.4.3 Melamine cabinets

Melamine cabinets can be painted with great success. The following steps can be followed:

Step 1 – Remove all the doors and drawers and start by removing the hardware and then cleaning it with a strong sugar soap solution. Neutralize the sugar soap by wiping it with a clean cloth soaked in clean water.

Step 2 – Lightly sand the doors and drawer fronts with a fine sand paper such as a 220 grit. Clean it with a damp cloth to remove dust. Remember to sand in the direction of the grain.

Step 3 – Apply a Melamine primer. Special primers are available for use on melamine, tiles etc.

Step 4 – When dry, sand down the primer lightly with a 220 grit sandpaper. Let it stand overnight to cure properly.

Step 5 – Apply at least two top coats of suitable water-based enamel paint.

Step 6 – Before replacing the doors, first paint the fixed units and make sure that all visible sections are painted. Use a high quality foam roller and follow the same procedure as described above.

When choosing paint for kitchen and bathroom cabinets, choose a specialized paint that can withstand high humidity and steam. Most of these paints also inhibit microbial growth, mould and mildew. It must also be washable and easy to clean.

5.5 How to stain wood

It is sometimes necessary to re-varnish a piece of furniture rather than to paint. This is especially true for antiques and some hardwood pieces such as Stinkwood and Yellow wood. Many clients prefer to keep the piece looking the same as the original. When the old finish has deteriorated and faded it is necessary to remove the old finish and start from scratch.

It is important to understand the difference between a stain, varnish and sealer.

A sealer penetrates into the wood and allows it to breathe and expand. It is not necessary to remove a sealer before refinishing wood.

A varnish forms a thin layer on the wood and does not penetrate. Old varnish must be removed totally before applying a new finish. It can be matt or gloss.

A stain colors the wood. It does not provide any protection to the wood and must be sealed to provide protection.

There are basically two types of stains – gel and liquid. They can also be water or oil-based   stains. The main reason for staining wood is to change or enhance the color:

Pine furniture can be turned into rich dark wood colors

Light woods can become dark woods

The color of weathered wood can be enhanced.

Gel stains are easy to apply. Use a lint free cloth or sponge to wipe on the wood. Liquid stains can be applied with a cloth or a brush.

To get a darker shade, apply more coats. Use plastic gloves to protect your hands. Remember that the stain does not protect the wood. When it is completely dry, finish it off with the application of a Polyurethane water-base sealer.

5.6 How to apply varnish and sealers to wood

Applying varnish and sealers is very straight forward. Just follow the manufacturer's instructions on the container. Always work in the direction of the grain. The surface must be well sanded, clean and free from dirt and grease. The best way to apply a varnish is to spray it. This gives a smooth, professional finish. Most varnishes are quick drying. At least two to three coats are required.

Varnishes come in different colors and are also available as a clear coating. They are also available in water-based or oil-based products.

A wide variety of sealers are available and I would recommend using a clear water-based sealer with a Polyurethane base. They are available in matt, gloss or sheen finish. I prefer the sheen finish for furniture.

5.7 Types of Paint

When you start out with the business of refinishing furniture, it is not always clear what type of paint will be most suitable for the job. To begin with, you have a choice between oil based and water based paint. Also there are so many paint manufacturers and they each claim to have the best product on the market. However, not all paints are the same. This is a costly lesson that I learned early on. I prefer to stick to the one or two of the larger manufacturers and to work with the same brand. This way you get to know the paint and how it will react to different wood surfaces.

5.7.1 Oil and Water based paints

Basically there are two types of paint. Water based paint which is also known as Latex or Acrylic paint. Oil based paint also known as Alkyd paint.

Latex paint was developed many years ago, using the resin of the rubber tree as a binder, known as Latex. Later years the original resin was replaced by a synthetic binder and it became known as Acrylic paint. Acrylic paint is made with water and an acrylic resin binder. Oil based paint uses an oil based solvent and an alkyd resin. It was originally made with linseed oil as a binder. That is why it was called "oil based" and although these days a synthetic resin is used, the name "oil based" remains. Thirty years ago, the manufacturing processes were not as good as they are with today's water based paint. The water paint manufactured today is as good as any oil based paint and in many ways is superior to the oil based paint. Today the surface of the water base paint is extremely durable and resists scuffs and scratches, has very good breathability and provides superior adhesion to the surface to be painted. After the paint has cured, it remains flexible which means that it will expand or contract with changes in temperature. Because it is porous, it allows moisture to escape from the paint surface. Another big advantage of water based paints is that has virtually no odor – which means low VOC (Volatile Organic Compound) and therefore less damage to the environment. It is much kinder to your health than oil based paint. Because it is water based, equipment can easily be cleaned with water. However, when fully cured, water will not clean equipment and thinners will have to be used. Lastly, water based paint is non-flammable.

Water based paint can be thinned with water and it can easily be sprayed provided that you use a nozzle of between 1.8 and 2mm.

Disadvantages of water based paints are:

On new wood a primer must first be used before painting

It sometimes raises the grain of the wood. This can be overcome by first applying a suitable wood sealer

Does not adhere to chalky surfaces

It cannot readily be painted over surfaces previously painted with oil-based paints. This can be overcome by sealing the old finish first.

Takes long to properly cure and can easily be damaged when not cured properly.

Advantages of water based paint are the following:

Quick drying resulting in better productivity:

Virtually no odor and low VOC (volatile organic compound) with less harm to the environment and your health

Paint is flexible and expands with temperature. Will not crack or flake

Equipment can be cleaned with water

Modern water based enamel paint will provide the same smooth, hard finish that could in the past only be achieved by oil paint.

Oil based paint on the other hand, has in the past been the preferred paint for many painters and the main reason was that the hard, durable finish resist scratches and is not affected by water or moisture. Oil-based paints use thinners (petrochemical distillate) as the solvent. That is why oil based paints are flammable and toxic. Latex paints use water as the primary vehicle which makes them much less hazardous. Sometimes oil based paints are also referred to as Alkyd paints. Alkyd is the term used for a synthetic resin. This means that it is a man made oil and it's not manufactured from plants or petroleum.

Advantages of alkyd/oil paints are the following:

Alkyd goes on smoother than water based paint but takes much longer to dry.

It gives a hard, durable finish that resist scratches and abrasions

Alkyd paint goes on smoother but has a much longer drying time as this paint needs to dry over a longer time period of up to 3 days.

Alkyd enamels are easy to wash because the surface is much harder than latex paint.

Alkyd paints are more chemically resistant to stand up to washing detergents than latex.

When running your hand over an oil paint, the texture will feel smoother than a latex paint (which almost always has a rubbery feel). However, modern water-based enamel paints have the same smooth texture as oil paint.

Disadvantages of oil based paints:

White oil paint will tend to turn yellow over time

Does not resist mildew that may form in high humidity areas

Has high VOC and is increasingly being replaced by water based paints

Strong odor that lasts for a long time

Does not "breath" like water based paint and as a result tend to crack, form bubbles or peal.

Has a very long drying time (up to 16 – 24 hours)

5.7.2 Chalk paint and milk paint

Chalk paint (and to a lesser extent, milk paint), has become very popular with DIY enthusiasts. Annie Sloan has developed this very successful chalk paint and is available in most specialized paint shops. It is widely used for distressing furniture because it is easily applied and easily sanded to reveal the base coat. It is a water-based ultra matt paint and dries very quickly. Although sanding of the old finish is said to be unnecessary, I have found that it sometimes shows yellow blotches on old varnished or painted wood as soon as the top coat is sealed with the wax or a water-based sealer. Another disadvantage is that it is very expensive and that the cost becomes prohibitive when doing larger pieces of furniture.

As an alternative, you could make your own chalk paint. It is really easy and it can be made at a fraction of the cost of commercial paints.

Here is what you will need:

Ultra matt Acrylic paint (paint used for walls and ceilings)

Interior crack filler

Water

Mix the ingredients in a suitable container as follows:

Step1 – Pour 1 cup of clean water into the container

Step 2 – Slowly add 1 cup of Crack Filler into the water and stir until smooth

Step 3 – Now add 2 cups of paint to the mixture. Add slowly and stir constantly to get a lump free mixture.

When spraying or brushing chalk paint on old furniture (painted or varnished), I use the following procedure:

Clean the wood with sugar soap to remove dirt

Sand to get a smooth finish

Seal the wood with a water-based sealer.

Apply final coats (at least 2)

If yellow spots still show through, apply another coat of sealer and re-paint

When the final coat is dry, seal with matt sealer.

To get a smooth finish, sand between coats with 220 grit sand paper.

When applying the paint, water can be added to thin the paint if necessary. Do not dilute more than 10%. Because of the nature of chalk paint, it takes some time to get use to working with it.

CHAPTER 6 - PAINT TECHNIQUES

A wide variety of decorative paint techniques can be used on furniture. I only want to cover some of the easier and more popular techniques. Most of these techniques are done by hand with brushes and rollers. It takes some practice to master some of them, but it will be worthwhile to get the hang of it since this will give you a competitive edge over your competitors. It also opens up other avenues that your business can develop into, such as training clients to use these techniques.

The following techniques will be discussed:

White wash technique

Distressing

Antiquing

Glazing

Dragging

Apart from the above, there are more advanced techniques such as:

Gilding – the application of gold, silver or platinum leaf to furniture

Verdigris – This refers to the green color of aged copper and is popular on wrought iron furniture. It can also be applied on wood.

Marbling - This is a technique to imitate the effect of marble on wooden countertops or other surfaces where marble can be found such as floors.

Stencils – use of stencils to transfer images onto wood

Decoupage

Wallpaper

More information about these techniques can readily be found on the internet.

6.1 White wash technique

White washing furniture has become very popular. By spray painting with a water-based paint, a very smooth and professional look is possible. It is also very fast and you can be sure that the end product will be very pleasing. The wood must be prepared by sanding it to get a bare wood surface. The paint is applied very thinly to reveal some of the bare wood.

The following materials are needed:

Off-white matt Acrylic paint

Water based clear varnish (matt)

Sand paper - 220grit and 360grit

Wood filler

Paint remover

Dry cloth

Preparation

Depending on the state of the piece of furniture, you will have to prepare it by doing the following:

Remove all hardware from the piece of furniture

Remove old paint or varnish by sanding with 220 grit sandpaper

If necessary, use water-based paint stripper to remove stubborn varnish or paint. Remember to neutralize the paint stripper with a wet cloth when finished.

If necessary, fill small nicks and scratches with wood filler and sand down to a smooth finish

When bare wood is visible, finish off with 360 grit sand paper to get smooth surface

When the preparation is complete, wipe down the piece to make sure that no dust or grit remains. You can now proceed with spray painting. The process is as follows:

Seal the wood with one coat of water - based varnish

When dry, flatten unevenness with 360 grit sand paper to a smooth finish

Dilute paint with water - 20% water

Spray lightly over whole piece of furniture

Try and avoid praying edges too heavily

After painting leave for at least 12 hours to completely dry the paint. Now the fun part starts. Sand down certain areas and edges with 360 grit sand paper to expose wood surface.

The last step is to seal the piece with water-based clear varnish. I find that at least 2 coats are needed to get a nice finish. It should be noted that not all wood is suitable for washing. Pine has a nice solid wood grain that shows up nicely when sanded and lends itself to white washing.

Tip: Always work along with the grain of the wood and try to avoid circular movements.

As an alternative, the above technique can be slightly changed to get an ***aged wash*** look. The process is as follows:

Open the grain of the wood by using a wire brush and removing the soft part of the wood and thus exposing the grain more prominently.

Then apply the diluted Acrylic paint with a brush and while the paint is still wet, use a big scraper to scrape off excess paint and leaving the remainder.

When dry, seal the paint with a matt water-based sealer.

Universal undercoat can also be used instead of Acrylic paint. Mix 2 parts of universal under coat with 1 part mineral turpentine and apply as set out above. When dry, seal with a water-based sealer.

6.2 Shabby chic

Shabby chic is actually not only a paint technique but it also refers to a decor style. It is an interior design where furniture is distressed to show wear and tear. Colors are mainly in white and soft pastel colors. Furniture that is mostly not genuine but resembles antique pieces is popular because it can be made to resemble old pieces by distressing and painting techniques. Cottage style decor enhances the shabby chic look.

To achieve the shabby chic look, the furniture is only lightly distressed and the top coat is usually in white, off-white or soft pastel colors.

The steps to follow to achieve a shabby chic look are the following:

Step 1 – prepare the wood for painting by cleaning and sanding the piece where necessary

Step 2 – Apply an undercoat

Step 3 – Apply a dark brown or graphite color at the edges.

The dark color can be applied liberally on edges.

Step 4 – Paint the whole piece of furniture with the first top coat – in this case in white or off-white. While the paint is still wet, take a cloth and remove the paint from the edges to show the dark color as shown below.

Step 5 – Apply a second and final top coat, again covering the whole piece of furniture. While the paint is still wet, take a cloth and very gently wipe away some of the paint at the edges. This step is aimed at getting a very soft distressed effect with a thin line of the dark color showing through.

Reduce dark color further to show thin lines

Note that the table is now very lightly distressed.

6.3 Distressing

Distressing of furniture is a relatively simple technique. The technique is much the same as described in the previous section. The aim is to take an older vintage piece of furniture in solid wood (veneers and compressed wood are not suitable for this technique) and distress it to emphasize the worn look. Any color can be used and the darker color is mostly used as the base coat but it depends on personal taste and preference.

There are mainly two types of distressing. The first is where the original bare wood is exposed under the top coat and the second where a base color is coated over with the a different color top coat and then rubbed away at points of natural wear and tear to expose the base coat. You also have the choice to distress heavily by even lightly damaging the wood with scratches and dents (even holes), or a light distress where a softer more elegant look is achieved. The process is the same as for preparing and painting any other piece of furniture.

When the objective is to expose the original wood, the piece must first be thoroughly sanded until the wood is exposed. If the wood surface seems to be dull an option is to first use an appropriate wood stain to color the wood to a more striking appearance.

The next step will be to paint the top coat in such a way that it can be sanded in certain areas to expose the wood surface. Before painting, apply a petroleum product such as Vaseline to the areas to be exposed such as edges, corners and around drawer handles. It can also be applied on flat areas. Be careful not to touch areas not to be distressed. Spray the first coat. You will notice that the paint does not stick properly to the Vaseline areas. This is good because this is where you want to distress the wood. Wait until the paint has dried and then sand to remove the paint on the Vaseline areas to expose the bare wood. To get a softer distressed look, you could wipe the paint when it is still wet.

For the color look, paint a base coat and when it is dry, apply Vaseline or candle wax to the areas to be distressed. Then paint the second color and when the paint dries, rub with steel wool over the waxed areas. The steel wool won't harm the rest of the paint but will help to find the waxed areas. Remember, the piece is meant to be distressed. Finally, seal the paint with a clear water-based paint sealer.

6.4 Antiquing natural wood surfaces

A wood surface can be aged (and then kept in its natural wood color) or it can be antiqued to imitate an antique or vintage piece of furniture.

Aging of wood can be done chemically and/or mechanically. Chemical treatment can easily be done with your own home made mixture of vinegar and steel wool.

To add an ashy or gray hue (to mimic sun fading); fill a spray bottle halfway with white vinegar. Then shred one pad of steel wool and push it into the spray bottle. Let the bottle sit in a warm sunny area for at least 3 to 4 hours and then spray its contents onto the wood and allow it to dry. Age, species, surface cut and sap content of wood will affect the process, so experiment with the amount of steel wool in the bottle, the amount of time the solution soaks and the number of coats applied. Always do a test piece first and stop applying solution when the wood achieves a color that is slightly lighter than the desired hue; the aging process will continue for a short while after drying.

Mechanical aging can be done by using a wire brush and pulling it along the grain of the wood to open the wood grain. A hammer chisel can be used to imitate deeper scratch marks or marks and dents on the edge of a table top. A chain can even be used to gently hit the wood surface to great dents.

6.5 Antiquing painted surfaces

Antiquing with two paint colors can best be done by using a process as follows:

6.5.1 Sanding and preparing

First the wood should be cleaned and sanded to expose the bear wood. An electric sander can be used to speed up the process. Sharp edges can be distressed by slightly flattening the sides. Take the opportunity to roughen the flat areas in selected spots to imitate normal wear and tear.

6.5.2 Prime the wood

After cleaning the wood with a cloth, the next step is to apply a white wood primer or undercoat. Use a sponge roller to apply the paint. Next, apply a top coat of off-white paint. While the paint is still wet, take a paint brush and lightly paint again to eliminate roller marks and to create brush marks, which is a more traditional effect for old painted furniture.

6.5.3 Re-sand the wood

To give the wood a more weathered look, use the sander to re-sand the surface. To distress the finish concentrate on areas that are naturally exposed to handling and remove the paint until the bare wood becomes visible. The effect can be subtle or more dramatic depending on your choice.

6.5.4 Apply stain

To get an antique look, apply a suitable stain such as antique oak or similar. This will provide a distressed vintage look. By applying more coats the finish will become darker. By applying more stain in certain areas a more distressed look will be achieved.

6.5.5 Apply Polyurethane sealer

The last step is to apply a clear polyurethane sealer to seal the stain and to protect the paint surface. A foam brush will make the application much more even.

6.5.6 Antiquing recipe

A popular technique is to use a ready-made antique glaze and applying it to crevices and molded areas to create an antique look. These glazes usually come in colors of umber and burnt sienna and are painted over a white or off-white base coat. Bold colors such as black, blue or olive green are also used.

The greater the contrast between base and the glaze, and the brighter the glaze color, the more obvious it will be that the piece of furniture is antiqued. If you're working over an existing finish, make sure the glaze is compatible.

Work on small areas at a time. Apply the glaze on molded areas and before it dries, use a clean cloth to wipe away some of the glaze. Move to the next section and repeat the process. Do not mess too much with the first application. Rather wait for it to dry and then apply another coat to get a deeper color.

Recipe for antiquing old furniture with two paint colors

This is a recipe with Plascon's paint products. You will need the following:

Plascon Universal undercoat

Plascon Double Velvet (Off-white - Grecian White VEL-33)

Plascon Double Velvet (Chocolate brown - Burro Bridge SJ-8)

Plascon Acrylic Scumble

Plascon Glaze coat (Matt)

Sugar soap and 220 and 600 grit sand paper, 50 mm paint brush, sponge rollers and tray and mutton cloth

The method is as follows:

Wash the wood with sugar soap and wipe it clean with water to neutralize the sugar soap

Sand with 220 grit sandpaper to a smooth finish

Apply one coat of universal undercoat

Apply base coat (2) of Double Velvet in Grecian White

Mix the Burro Bridge with the acrylic scumble and water to the ratio of 1:1:1

Apply the mixture to selected areas such as moldings, carvings etc.

Finish the paint with 2 layers of Glaze Coat to get a smooth matt finish

Tip: sand lightly between each layer with a fine sand paper (600grit) or sanding sponge.

6.6. Glazing

Glazing is a technique that is used by furniture makers to add color to finished natural wood products. It is applied between the layers of finish. It is different from staining in that stain is applied to raw wood and the stain penetrates the wood. It is very difficult to remove the stain once it is dry. Glaze is applied to wood that has at least one layer of finish such as varnish or paint. The glaze does not penetrate the wood and is much more controllable. It can be removed and the process can be repeated until the desired finish is obtained.

Glazing can be done in several ways. Firstly, a glaze can be used to provide a protective finish over paint techniques and can be matt, gloss or sheen. Secondly, glazing is done to achieve an antique look to a piece of furniture.

6.7 Sealing paint techniques with glaze

This is a very simple process. When the paint effect is done, use an oil- or water-based clear glaze to seal the paint work. It takes a while to completely cure and care must be taken not to put heavy objects on the surface for at least 3 – 5 days. A glaze sealer comes in matt or gloss. It is actually a varnish and forms a thin layer on the paint work that protects the paint from scratches, water and rough handling. To make your own color, combine glazing medium with your paint (either latex or acrylic). Generally the ratio is four parts glaze to one part paint, but you should follow the manufacturer's instructions.

The amount of glazing medium you add to the paint can affect the color of the glaze. When you're using lighter paint colors, a 4-to-1 mixture will not affect the color. But darker colors may be altered to a lighter color value when mixed with too much glaze. The translucency of the glaze is determined by how much paint you add. More paint than glaze results in less translucency; less paint than glaze results in more translucency.

You apply glaze just as you would apply paint, with a brush or roller or by spraying it. Again, work in small sections: roll on the glaze, finish the technique and then move on to the next section. And if you're doing a two-person job, make sure one person is always rolling and the other is working with the glaze. That will give you the most consistent treatment.

Drying time for glaze varies; usually you have about 10 to 20 minutes to work with the glaze before it dries completely. To increase the drying time, add a paint extender such as Plascon's scumble glaze to your mixture. It's possible to create beautiful paint treatments using glaze. Just remember:

Paint on a semi gloss surface.

Mix glaze to the right translucency and consistency.

Work in small sections.

Antique glazing

Look for transparent antiquing glaze, in muted tones of umber and burnt sienna or in white, gold, black, or colors.

To apply glaze, the following steps can be used:

Glaze can be added to paint to extend the drying time – this will give you more time to work with your glaze.

Water-based glazes and paints are the easiest to work with and to clean up.

Glazes can be bought ready mixed in different colors, or you can make up your own glaze color.

The following equipment will be needed:

Two paint brushes. One to apply the glaze and a dry brush to blend the glaze to get an even distribution of glaze and to remove air bubbles.

Paper towels to wipe the glaze

Steel wool to remove excess glaze and to tone the color

The process is to apply the glaze, wipe some off and then blend and remove if necessary. If things go wrong, simply take a damp cloth, wipe the glaze and start again.

6.8 Special effects with glaze

Different colors can be used to obtain dramatic effects. For instance use a bold color such as blue or olive green and apply a black glaze. By using steel wool or nylon pads, carvings and recessed corners can be highlighted by rubbing off glaze from the highest areas. On a table top the edges can be a bit darker and lighter towards the centre.

White washing light grained wood such as pine can be very effective with a white or off-white glaze. When mixed with emulsion paint like Plascon Double Velvet, for example, it may be applied over a base coat of another color, and patterned to reveal the color below.

When mixed with colored paint, it may be sanded to create a matt, chalky surface or it can be lightly dragged with a dry brush to reveal thin striped effect.

6.8.1 Dragging

This is a process of dragging on wood is done to reveal thin stripes of a slightly darker shade on a base coat. The dry brush technique is used where one brush is used to apply the base coat in the normal way and a second darker color is applied in thin stripes.

Recipe for dragging on wood:

The following paint (all Plascon products) can be used:

Double Velvet Happy Ending (Y5-B2-3) – off – white color

Double Velvet Fresh Linen (E3-Y2-3) – green/grey color

Plascon Glaze Coat (mat)

The procedure is as follows:

Sand the wood and apply one coat of universal undercoat

Paint the Happy Ending at least two coats

When dry, brush the Fresh Linen lightly dragging thin lines in a vertical direction over the base coat

Do only a small area at a time and while the paint is still wet, take a dry brush and wipe off some of the wet paint in the same direction to leave faint stripes

When dry, apply two coats of Glaze Coat to seal the paint.

As an alternative, a glaze can be added to the paint as indicated below.

Step 1 – Mix the glaze with one part of the darker color paint, one part paint, one part water and one part scumble glaze. Use the mixing brush to apply a thin layer of glaze over the top coat.

Step 2 – While the glaze is still wet, gently pull a piece of mutton cloth over the surface in a vertical direction. Do not lift the cloth.

Step 3 – Now do the same with a clean brush. Work steadily before the glaze is completely dry. Allow it to dry for 24 hours, and seal the paint with a clear sealer such as Plascon's Glaze Coat. The same technique can be used to create a wood grain effect by combing a brown glaze over the painted surface.

Step 4 - For a more rustic look, take a piece of 150 grit sand paper and drag in the direction of the lines. Dust with a dry brush and seal with a sealer.

CHAPTER 7 - HOW TO GROW YOUR BUSINESS

Since the aim of the book is to help you to create a profitable home business, this chapter deals with the basic requirements to get started. I have gone through the same process and although I have made some mistakes along the way, my experience was that there is a ready market out there that just needs to be to be explored. In this chapter I share my experience with you and give some guidelines to follow to assist you in the process of building a viable home business.

7.1 How to find a market

When you feel that you are ready to start taking on assignments, you will have to develop a market for your services.

The most effective approach is to identify potential customers and to approach them directly. Apart from private customers, there are some businesses that will make use of painting and restoration services.

7.1.1 Interior designers

Interior designers and decorators can be a good source of income for your business. In many cases a client's old furniture need refinishing or painting to fit in with the new design. If you can build a good relationship with an internal design business, you will have a constant supply of work. The most important factor for success is to provide a professional service. Quality is crucial. Personal contact is essential because this will help you to identify your customer's needs. Once you know what that is, focus your efforts on satisfying that need. I have a long standing relationship with an interior designer who also sells Annie Sloan chalk paint. I realized that if I could develop an expertise in spraying chalk paint both of us will benefit (see par 5.7.2).

7.1.2 Kitchen cabinet manufacturers

Painted kitchen cabinets have become very popular and most progressive cabinet manufacturers now provide clients with this option. Melamine cabinets have become old fashioned and MDF (Supawood) is used to create unique cabinet styles that can be painted in any color or paint technique applications. The fact is that painting and more specifically spray painting is something that they are not familiar with and in most cases will gladly outsource this function - especially small and medium size businesses.

The main obstacle is to convince a potential client that you can provide a professional service at a competitive price. The best way to do this is to provide examples of your work in MDF. As far as pricing is concerned, remember that the best way is to agree on a price per square meter. This way the manufacturer can add it to his manufacturing cost and get a comparable price for melamine or any other alternative.

The advantage of this approach is that even if you have to cut your price to the bone, you will have a constant flow of work that will enable you to expand your business. Spraying MDF is a pleasure and because most of the spraying is done on smooth and flat surfaces, it is fast and effective.

7.1.3 Antique and second hand furniture dealers

These days many furniture dealers see an opportunity to diversify their business by adding painted furniture to their product range. In some instances they also need restoration services and refinishing of items. Again the price that you can charge is usually not as high as with private customers, but if a constant supply of work can be obtained, it becomes a viable proposition.

7.1.4 Private customers

Although it takes time to build a customer base, private customers are important because they provide a wide range of furniture pieces and gives you the opportunity to expand your expertise in different paint techniques. A decent price can also be charged and once you have built a good reputation, a constant supply of work will be assured.

7.2 How to cost projects

It is essential to cost projects on a fair and objective basis. This will ensure that prices are competitive and transparent. This will also make it easier to administer and to adjust your price when the price of consumables such as paint and other materials increases.

The costing of different types of furniture is can only be done effectively if the approach provides for the different types such as flat areas, small items, second hand or new etc..

7.2.1 Costing flat areas such as kitchen cabinets

When painting flat surfaces such as kitchen cabinets or tables, it makes sense to use the square area (square meter or feet) as a price unit. Items such as chairs are more difficult to price because it is difficult to calculate the squares and in many cases it does not give an accurate picture of the amount of work involved. It should also be remembered that amount of work involved can vary from piece to piece and depending on the amount of time spent on preparation, the price will be higher.

I have developed a format on a spreadsheet (Table 4) and for each project the following cost items are used:

The amount of paint needed (including primer, undercoat, sealer and top coat)

Other materials needed such as sand paper, wood filler, mineral turpentine etc

Labor cost including professional time and labor time (hourly basis)

Overheads and other costs such as transport.

Although **profit** is not a cost for the business, it needs to be included in the calculation of the price of a project. In the example below it is added to the project cost to get to the total project cost.

To calculate the ***volume of paint required***, the area of the object is calculated and then divided by the spreading rate times the number of coats. The cost is calculated by multiplying the paint cost with the volume required. Remember to round off the volume required to the nearest liter or other volume supplied by the store.

Other materials such as sand paper, filler etc is simply calculated as 15% of the total paint cost.

Labor cost is made up of the spray painter's cost as 85% of the total material cost. Laborer cost is based on the number of hours estimated for the project times the hourly rate.

Overhead cost depends on cost items such as rent, electricity etc. And each case will be different. In my case I have estimated that with the value of the average number of jobs per month, about 10% of the material cost will cover my overheads.

Profit is calculated at 15% of the total project cost.

The Cost Calculator

In table 4 the Cost Calculator is used to calculate the costs to paint kitchen cabinets.

To use this cost calculator is easy because the only ***variables*** that need to be adjusted for each project are the following:

Area of the items to be painted

Other costs such as transport or repairs where they are applicable (travel distance, no of hours required for repairs etc.)

The price of paint to be adjusted when necessary.

The Cost Calculator can be developed as an Excel document and used as a template for your costing activities.

Table 4 – Cost Calculator –total paint costs

PROJECT:	Kitchen cabinets				Area 8.16m²
PAINT MATERIALS	Stripper	Undercoat	Top coat	Sealer	Total
Price per liter	R150.00	R 120.00	R150.00	R150.00	
Area - sq m	8.16	8.16	8.16	8.16	
No of coats	0.00	1.00	2.00	0.00	
Coverage per m²	6.00	5.00	8.00	8.00	
Liters needed	0.00	1.63	2.04	0.00	
Liters to purchase	0.00	2.0	2.00	0.00	
Total paint cost	R -	R 240.00	R300.00	R -	R540.00

Total paint cost includes all paint, stripper, sealers etc. and is based on the liters required to cover the area of the object to be painted.

Table 5 – Total other material cost

OTHER MATERIALS					
Other materials - 10% of paint cost					R 81.00
Total other material cost					R621.00

Other materials such as sand paper, masking tape etc. To simplify the calculation, a figure of 10% of paint costs. This can be adjusted if required.

Table 6 – Total labor cost

LABOR COST	Hrs				
Painter- 85 % of material					R527.85
Laborer - R18.75/hour	5.00				R 93.75
Total labor cost					**R621.60**

Labor cost for a specialized spray painter can be calculated at an hourly rate or as in this case as a percentage of material cost.

Table 7 – Others costs

OTHER COSTS	Hrs	Distance			
Transport- R1.50 per km		0.00			R -
Repair work - R50 per hour	0.00				R -
Overhead cost - 10% of material cost					R 62.10
Total other costs					**R 62.10**

Other costs such as transport and repair work are calculated at a fixed rate. With a home business you do not necessarily have many overheads such as rent, telephone etc. and to simplify the calculation, a percentage of material cost is used.

Table 8 – Total project cost

PROJECT COST					R1,304.70
PROFIT 15%					R 195.71
TOTAL PROJECT COST					**R1,500.41**

A profit of 15% is added to project cost to get a total project cost.

Table 9 – Cost analysis

ANALYSIS					
Material as % of total cost					41%
Labor as % of total cost					41%
Other costs as % of total cost					4%
Total cost/ m²					R 183.95
SUMMARY	Labor	Material	Other cost	Profit	Total
Cabinets	R621.60	R 621.00	R 62.10	R195.71	R1,500.41

An analysis of the cost ratio of materials, labor and other costs gives an indication of their contribution towards the total project cost. The cost per square meter is an important indicator that can be used to compare different jobs and to serve as a yard stick for costing projects. It can also be used to compare competitor prices.

7.2.2 Costing furniture

When it comes to furniture, it can be more difficult to calculate costs involved because it is sometimes more difficult to calculate the area. The amount of preparatory work could also affect the unit price (R/sq m). Flat furniture such as tables and cabinets do not present any difficulty, but when you deal with items such as cane chairs or slatted head boards it requires adjustments.

To make it easy, I treat such items the same as flat objects because when you spray a cane chair for instance, the amount of paint will be the same as for a flat surface since much of the paint spray will pass through the openings and will thus be used as if it is sprayed on a flat surface.

As a guideline, the table (10) below shows price ranges for major furniture items.

Table 10 – Guideline prices for furniture

ITEM	LOW	HIGH	AVE
Chairs	R 200	R 350	R 280
Coffee tables	R 250	R 350	R 300
Dining room tables	R 700	R1200	R 900
Chest of drawers	R900	R1800	R1400
Cabinets / wardrobes	R 1 500	R2500	R2000
Trunks	R 800	R1200	R1000

7.2.3 Costing small objects

When you deal with smaller items such as picture frames, chandeliers etc. price cannot be determined by using the area to be sprayed. The best option is to let the customer provide the paint and that you only charged for labor based on the estimated time involved. For larger items the Cost Calculator as set out in table 5 can be used to cost your projects. The basis on which it is based is the area of the item that needs to be painted. The calculation of the square meters of each item needs to be determined as accurately as possible. It is essential to measure each item and it is helpful to measure the different parts of a piece of furniture separately and then to get the total area.

Notes:

Liters paint to buy is rounded off to the nearest liter.

Material and labor costs are equal or close to equal

7.3 How to use the internet for marketing

The internet opens up a wide range of possibilities for marketing your services. Some of these options include the following:

Advertising free on websites such as Gumtree

Using social media such as Facebook, Twitter etc.

E mail marketing

Creating your own website or blog

7.3.1 Internet advertising

To use sites such as Gumtree is really very easy. The ads are free and posting can be done with minimum effort. Make sure that you have a good picture of your product.

7.3.2 Social media

When you join the *sales groups* on Facebook, you can showcase your products and sell them to people in your area. Paid ads can also be placed on Twitter and a click on the image will take the person straight to your website.

7.3.3 E-mail marketing

E-mail marketing can be very successful provided that you do not use an address without the permission of the owner and by so doing making yourself guilty of spamming. It takes time to build an e-mail list and it takes constant updating to keep it going. A good strategy to get e-mail addresses is to offer something for the use of the address. A free video for example, on an aspect of refinishing such as particular paint technique, can be used to get permission to use an e-mail address. Another option is to provide a regular news letter in exchange for the e-mail address.

7.3.4 Creating a website

This can be an expensive and time consuming project. I would suggest that you start off by creating a free blog on Blogger or Word Press. This will give you the opportunity to get the feeling of running a website. You could also use a free website provider such as Weebly to create a website. They will supply a domain name and hosting free of charge. You could hire a website creator to design and implement your website.

Once you have created your website, it should be updated regularly with fresh authentic content.

7.4 Develop a business plan

Since we are looking at a home business it could be argued that a business plan will not make a significant difference to the establishment of the business. The biggest advantage of a business plan is that it forces you to think through a process of how you visualize the development of the business. Like with any business, the aim is to grow the business and to make a decent profit. Setting attainable goals will help to achieve those aims.

When compiling a business plan, the following questions should be answered:

Why do I want to start a furniture refinishing business?

What will my business do to be different from the rest?

Who is the ideal customer?

What do you want to achieve in the first year?

What steps will you take to attain those goals?

What will it cost?

What will be your pricing strategy?

The final step is to do a SWOT analysis to identify strengths, weaknesses, opportunities and threats. This analysis will hopefully assist you to avoid future problems.

Why start a furniture refinishing business?

There could be many reasons for starting a business. You could be retired and want to supplement your pension or just to keep busy. Your strategy for the future of the business will depend heavily on what the answer is to these two alternatives. Maybe you know people in the furniture and/or cabinet manufacturing industries and this present an ideal opportunity to enter into an agreement to provide a refinishing and painting business. Maybe you have a passion for restoring old furniture to their former glory. Whatever the reason, think it through and write it down as a pointer of where you want to go with the business.

What will my business do to be different from the rest?

To compete effectively in the marketplace, your business should have unique selling points (USP's). Why would people want to use your business when there are others that have been around for a long time? Do you have unique skills or do you use more sophisticated paint techniques? Can you supply a range of products and services that make yours different from the others?

There are some big and established businesses in the refinishing business and if you start out as a small business it will be almost impossible to compete with them That is why I suggest that you start small, keeping your overheads to the minimum. This will enable you to come in at a much lower price and by so doing get your foot in the door.

Who is the ideal customer?

By identifying the ideal customer, you can focus on your target market and not spend time or money on efforts that will not yield the required results. Having established your target market, a strategy can then be developed to make contact. There could be a number of ways to approach and convince the potential customer to use your services such as personal contact, regular e-mails, phone calls etc. Your program should not be a once off, but should be done on a continuously and regular basis.

What do you want to achieve in the first year?

By setting some goals to be achieved in the next 12 months, you can focus attention and resources to achieve them. Goals need not all be monetary. Aspects such as improving skills and techniques, penetrating a specific target market etc. are just as important.

What steps will you take to achieve those goals?

This is an obvious question to set the process in motion. Programs to consider are things like news paper ads, flyers, radio, internet marketing, e-mails, billboards, post, telephone etc.

Special promotions can be offered from time to time and the aim should be to expand your customer base and increasing sales.

What will it cost?

A budget should be drawn up and expenditure carefully monitored. Returns on the investment should also be established and monitored to see if the programs are meeting their goals.

What will be your pricing strategy?

Be aware of prices that are charged by competitors and make sure that your prices are competitive. Also consider the possibility to give discounts or other incentives such as free transport to special clients, especially if you want to establish a long term relationship.

7.5 Build a photo gallery and project data base

The only way you can show new customers what your work looks like, is by showing them pictures. The most effective way is to have before and after photos. Another important aspect is to make samples of paint techniques and to show some of the most popular paint color combinations. I made a number of wood panels about 25 cm x 25 cm and painted them in different paint techniques. These are very effective when customers have to decide on techniques and colors for kitchen cabinets, cupboards etc.

A project data base includes a short summary of each of your projects and contains information such as the following;

Short description and date of the project

Name and contact details of the customer

Type and color of paint that was used

Other relevant information

Publishing your photo gallery on the internet will increase views and make your website more interesting.

7.6 Estimated start up costs

Although start up costs can vary for different situations, I have tried to give an indication of what it will cost you to set up a small business. The prices may for tools and equipment may vary from location to location, but the aim is to show that with minimal capital outlay you can get the wheels in motion. With as little as R15000 or $1000 you can have a complete shop.

The table 10 below is a summary of the capital costs for tools and equipment.

Table 11– Estimated start up costs

Capital cost	*Amount	*USD	Other
Paint tools and equipment			
Compressor - 100 liter	R 4,000.00	260	
Spray guns 2mm & 1.4mm	R 1,200.00	80	
Respirator (3M) half mask	R 750.00	50	
Orbital sander	R 500.00	33	
Belt sander	R 700.00	45	
Heat gun	R 350.00	25	
Brushes and rollers	R 300.00	20	
Paint scrapers	R 100.00	10	
Paint strainers	R 100.00	10	
Paint mixing cups	R 100.00	10	
Sub-total	**R 8,100.00**	**543**	
Workshop equipment			
Saw horses and planks	R 1,500.00	100	
Clamps	R 800.00	55	
Planer	R 1,200.00	80	
Power drill	R 1,000.00	65	
Power screw driver	R 850.00	60	
Power saw	R 1,200.00	80	
Staple gun	R 350.00	25	

Sub-total	R 6,900.00	465	
TOTAL CAPITAL COST	R 15,000.00	1008	
*Note: Estimated values			

Most of the items mentioned can be purchased from hardware stores. You will probably already have many of the items and this will reduce your costs to a minimum. Furniture refinishing as a home business has very view risks and with minimum capital you can start a profitable business.

CHAPTER 8 - RESOURCES

In this chapter I will discuss the type of paints and other materials that I have found to be the best for spray painting furniture and cabinets. As was mentioned earlier, I work only with water based products and they are locally available from hardware stores. These products are all South African brands and not available in other countries.

8.1 Paints and primers

The main paint manufacturers that supply quality paints are the following:

Plascon Paint

Dulux Paint

Duram Paint

8.2 Primers/under coats

Although all paint manufacturers have good water based wood primers, I use *Plascon Multi-Surface Primer*. It can be used on other surfaces such as melamine, tiles etc. and come at a very competitive price. It can be thinned at 10% with water but when stirred properly, it can be sprayed without thinning. Dulux Paints has *Super Grip All Surface Primer* that can also be used.

8.3 Paints

Again, all the bigger paint manufacturers have excellent quality paints but for top coats I prefer to use *Plascon's Velvaglo water based enamel paint*. Although it is non-drip paint and therefore very thick, it can be thinned with water up to 15%. When you are going to do a paint technique and more than one color is used, there is usually a fair amount of sanding and I suggest that *Double*

Velvet from Plascon be used for this purpose. It is much easier to sand and it seals well.

Pearglo from Dulux also sprays well but is much more expensive than Plascon.

Duram makes very tough water based enamel paint (*Nu Glo*) and I use it when I need a really durable finish. It has Polyurethane added and is scratch and stain resistant.

When painting furniture or cabinets for kitchens or bathrooms, I suggest that the special paints developed by Plascon, Duram or Dulux be used. These paints have been specifically manufactured for kitchen and bathroom surfaces and are 10 times more washable than other water based paints.

8.4 Stains and waxes

I recommend using *Woodoc* for treating natural hardwood furniture. Woodoc's range of gel stains are easy to use and come in a range of natural wood colors as well as a clear finish. Their furniture wax comes in a liquid and paste. The greatest advantage of their products is that it penetrates into the wood and does not form a layer on top of the surface that can be scratched like ordinary wood varnish. It comes in gloss, sheen and matt.

8.5 Wood reviver

Weathered or blackened wood can be renovated with Woodoc's *Wood Reviver*. It is a powerful wood cleaner and is ideal for bleaching wood to remove black spots.

Tip: Black spots on wood are a sign of fungal growth and must be removed before the wood start rotting.

8.6 Wood Sealers

When paint techniques are used such as white wash or distressing, it is advisable to seal the finish with a sealer to protect the top coat. The sealers used on bare wood surfaces do not work well on painted surfaces and I suggest a water based, clear sealer such as Plascon's Glaze coat that has specifically been developed for paint effects.

8.7 Paint Stripper

I have tried a number of paint strippers and prefer to use *RemovAll* from Plascon. It is a water based paint stripper that will almost all paint and varnished finishes. It is brush able but will stick to vertical surfaces. It has virtually no smell and can easily be removed with water when it comes into contact with the skin.

8.8 Tools and equipment

All of the tolls and equipment can be bought from any hardware store. Compressors can be very expensive and I suggest that you buy imported Chinese products. These are just as good as the local machines but much cheaper. Be aware that you buy from a reputable dealer so that you will be able to buy spares and maintenance items locally.

CONCLUSION

Refinishing furniture has become increasingly popular and it presents an ideal opportunity for anybody to enter this market. It is particularly suitable as a home business because it can be started on a small scale and as experience is gained and a client base is established the business can gradually be developed to a profitable small business.

To be successful, the most important factor is to provide a quality service. Even though you might start out small and only use brushes and rollers to apply the paint, your service must become more professional and that is why I emphasize the use of spray painting equipment to apply paint. The investment you make in quality will pay off and whether you do it as a part time business or as a full time home business, you will earn a really good income from your efforts.

Printed in Great Britain
by Amazon